RUTH
An Interlinear Hebrew Translation Workbook

Also from Alef Press:

Biblical Hebrew: A Homeschool Primer: a thorough and encouraging guide to reading and writing Biblical Hebrew for ages 9 and up with creative exercises, traditional music, an introduction to grammar and vocabulary, and a dash of fun for high school foreign language credits and lifelong Bible study

Biblical Hebrew: Annotations and Answers: the essential teacher's manual designed to accompany the primer with answers, details, suggestions for use and supplemental resources, and an original audio CD of traditional Hebrew songs

Biblical Hebrew: Show and Tell: DVD supplement to the primer with engaging and insightful stories from history and tradition illustrated by photos of places and wildlife in Israel, Biblical sites, art and artifacts; pronunciation of each lesson; and audiovisual review

Jonah Copybook, Malachi, and Ruth: These interlinear Hebrew translation workbooks comprise the complete (unaccented) Biblical text of respectively, the books of Jonah, Malachi, and Ruth, with word-for-word English rendering, and instructions and space for copywork and translation. **Malachi** and **Ruth** include helpful grammar and translation notes. These workbooks, designed for use as copybooks by beginners and translation help for more advanced students, can supplement any Biblical Hebrew course.

Biblical Hebrew 2: A high school level course for lifelong learning from God's Word designed for Christian families and schools. Besides the grammar and vocabulary necessary to read most of the Hebrew Bible, *Biblical Hebrew 2* offers tools and background for a lifetime of vibrant and practical Bible study with explorations of manuscript history and reliability, Hebrew wordplay, archaeological discoveries, challenges and methods of translation, Hebrew's modern revival in Israel, Biblical poetry, the Talmud, Jewish Bible study traditions, textual criticism, literary devices, and how to conduct a contextual word study using Hebrew.

Biblical Hebrew 2 Workbook: Student workbook with a year and a half of daily exercises, tailored to the textbook lessons, in reading, understanding, and translating Biblical Hebrew. *Biblical Hebrew 2 Workbook Answer Key*: Full-size, completed workbook edition

RUTH
An Interlinear Hebrew Translation Workbook

Kim McKay

ALEF PRESS

Alef Press

1036 Chestnut Hill Road
Cambridge, New York 12816
USA
www.alefpress.org

COPYRIGHT © 2014 by Kim McKay

All rights reserved. No part of this publication may be reproduced, stored in a retrieval system, or transmitted in any form or by any means, including photocopying, without permission of the publisher.

ISBN: 978-0-9881738-9-7

ART CREDITS: Cover painting by Camille Pissarro, 1880, courtesy National Gallery of Art, Washington, D.C.; wheat icon courtesy Freepik from Flaticon.com

TRANSLATION CREDITS: Scripture quotations marked (ESV) are from The Holy Bible, English Standard Version® (ESV®), copyright © 2001 by Crossway Bibles, a publishing ministry of Good News Publishers. Used by permission. All rights reserved. THE HOLY BIBLE, NEW INTERNATIONAL VERSION®, NIV® Copyright © 1973, 1978, 1984, 2011 by Biblica, Inc.™ used by permission. All rights reserved worldwide. Scripture taken from GOD'S WORD®, © 1995 God's Word to the Nations used by permission of Baker Publishing Group. Scripture citations from the Douay-Rheims Bible and King James Version are in the public domain. Quotations marked NETS are taken from A New English Translation of the Septuagint, ©2007 by the International Organization for Septuagint and Cognate Studies, Inc. Used by permission of Oxford University Press. All rights reserved. Scripture quotations taken from the Holy Bible, New Living Translation, copyright ©1996, 2004, 2007, 2013 by Tyndale House Foundation used by permission of Tyndale House Publishers, Inc., Carol Stream, Illinois 60188. All rights reserved. Scripture quotations marked HCSB are taken from the Holman Christian Standard Bible®, Copyright © 1999, 2000, 2002, 2003, 2009 by Holman Bible Publishers. Used by permission. Scripture taken from the NEW AMERICAN STANDARD BIBLE®, Copyright © 1960,1962,1963,1968,1971,1972,1973,1975,1977,1995 by The Lockman Foundation. Used by permission. Quotations designated (NET) are from the NET Bible® copyright ©1996-2006 by Biblical Studies Press, L.L.C. http://netbible.com All rights reserved.

Printed in the United States of America

INTRODUCTION

Ruth: An Interlinear Hebrew Translation Workbook comprises the complete (unaccented) Biblical text of the book of Ruth, a word-for-word rendering, and space for copywork and translation.

It can be used as a supplement to any Hebrew course, and by beginning and more advanced Hebrew students in different ways.

Students who have learned to pronounce and write Hebrew words can develop fluency and gain a foothold in grammar, syntax, idiom, and translation by reading aloud and copying the Hebrew, then translating from the provided English glosses. Beginners should, little by little, read aloud the text, copy the Hebrew words, and notice as much as possible about them and the English glosses. Reference charts for pronunciation and block and script handwriting are provided on pages 62 and 63. Copying vowels is optional. It becomes tedious, and vowel points are not used in most Hebrew writing, anyway.

Students of grammar who are ready to read meaningfully can cover the English words and write their own word-for-word translation in the boxes. They may wish to test themselves and use the provided English only as an answer key, or to take the opportunity to consult reference works and explore word meanings and idioms more fully, with the basic translations at hand. They can then write their own English translation straight from Scripture.

The Alef Press interlinear Hebrew translation workbooks differ from most interlinear Bible translations by smoothing out the Hebrew much less. We do not skip any words; when you read Scripture in Hebrew for yourself, you need to know what to make of each word. Here you get the practice and assistance to do just that.

We have purposefully chosen common, simple glosses that you are likely to have memorized, so that you can notice the figurative or extended meanings that arise from the simpler root, and become used to reading meaningfully in context with these words.

Next to each ear of grain is room for your own translation of that page. Word-for-word translation makes hash of Hebrew idiom and proper English. You will have the fun of sorting that out. If you get stuck, any English Bible can be consulted for ideas, and it may prove interesting to compare multiple versions. We have supplied grammatical and translation notes as an appendix beginning on page 64.

Ruth can be used at any stage of Hebrew learning, but in the Alef Press series of Biblical Hebrew resources, it is recommended for use after completion of the **Biblical Hebrew 2** textbook because the endnotes emphasize verb stems beyond qal to serve as a bridge from the textbook to further reading from Scripture. The verb stems and qualities are described in Chapter 44 of **Biblical Hebrew 2** and summarized here:

Qal, or *Pa'al*: simple action, active voice

Nifal: simple action, passive voice

Piel: intensive action, active voice

Pual: intensive action, passive voice

Hifil: causative action, active voice

Hofal: causative action, passive voice

Hitpael: intensive action, middle (reflective) voice

GRAMMAR NOTES FOR BEGINNERS

Readers who have not yet studied grammar should be aware of a few things before getting started:

• The verb "to be" is often implied rather than spoken in Hebrew. A Hebrew sentence that said, "God good" would be in English, "God is good."

• There is one word here that has no English equivalent and is represented in our English translation only by an arrow. This word precedes a definite direct object. For example, I ate → the cake. Word order cannot be depended upon to identify a direct object. If the Hebrew word order reads, "the prophet loved the LORD," look for the → to know whether the prophet loved → the LORD or the LORD loved → the prophet.

• The sacred Name of God, commonly represented by "the LORD" in English Bibles, is composed of the letters yud-hey-vav-hey. Its pronunciation is unknown and not attempted out of reverence. Where it appears with vowels, the vowels are only a reminder to substitute "Adonai," meaning "Lord."

• Capital letters are included in our English translation only following a sof-passuk. It is up to the translator to determine other sentence breaks in English.

• To say *this something*, Hebrew will say *the something the this*. On the first line of page 24 is an example: *the young woman the this* would be properly translated into English as *this young woman*.

PLEASE TURN THIS BOOK UPSIDE DOWN, AND TURN THE PAGE TO BEGIN RUTH IN HEBREW

Ruth 1: 1-2

רָעָב	וַיְהִי	הַשֹּׁפְטִים	שְׁפֹט	בִּימֵי	וַיְהִי
a famine	and it was	the judges	to judge	in the days of	And it was

יְהוּדָה	לֶחֶם	מִבֵּית	אִישׁ	וַיֵּלֶךְ	בָּאָרֶץ
Judah	bread	from the house of	a man	and walked	in the land

וּשְׁנֵי	וְאִשְׁתּוֹ	הוּא	מוֹאָב	בִּשְׂדֵי	לָגוּר
and the two of	and his wife	he	Moab	in the fields of	to sojourn

אִשְׁתּוֹ	וְשֵׁם	אֱלִימֶלֶךְ	הָאִישׁ	וְשֵׁם	בָּנָיו:
his wife	and the name of	Elimelech	the man	And the name of	his sons

וְכִלְיוֹן	מַחְלוֹן	בָּנָיו	שְׁנֵי-	וְשֵׁם	נָעֳמִי
and Chilion	Mahlon	his sons	the two of	and the name of	Naomi

שְׂדֵי-	וַיָּבֹאוּ	יְהוּדָה	לֶחֶם	מִבֵּית	אֶפְרָתִים
fields of	and they came	Judah	bread	from the house of	Ephrathites

אִישׁ	אֱלִימֶלֶךְ	וַיָּמָת	שָׁם:	וַיִּהְיוּ-	מוֹאָב
the husband of	Elimelech	And died	there	and were	Moab

וַיִּשְׂאוּ	בָנֶיהָ:	וּשְׁנֵי	הִיא	וַתִּשָּׁאֵר	נָעֳמִי
and they carried	her sons	and the two of	she	and was left	Naomi

Ruth 1:4-5

עָרְפָּה	הָאַחַת	שֵׁם	מֹאֲבִיּוֹת	נָשִׁים	לָהֶם
Orpah	the one	the name of	Moabitish	wives	to them

כְּעֶשֶׂר	שָׁם	וַיֵּשְׁבוּ	רוּת	הַשֵּׁנִית	וְשֵׁם
about ten	there	and they dwelt	Ruth	the second	and the name of

וְכִלְיוֹן	מַחְלוֹן	שְׁנֵיהֶם	גַּם־	וַיָּמוּתוּ	שָׁנִים:
and Chilion	Mahlon	both	also	And died	years

וַתָּקָם	וּמֵאִישָׁהּ:	יְלָדֶיהָ	מִשְּׁנֵי	הָאִשָּׁה	וַתִּשָּׁאֵר
And arose	and from her husband	her children	from two	the woman	and was left

כִּי	מוֹאָב	מִשְּׂדֵי	וַתָּשָׁב	וְכַלֹּתֶיהָ	הִיא
because	Moab	from the fields of	and returned	and her daughters-in-law	she

יְהוָה	פָּקַד	כִּי־	מוֹאָב	בִּשְׂדֵה	שָׁמְעָה
the LORD	attended to	that	Moab	in the fields of	she heard

וַתֵּצֵא	לָחֶם:	לָהֶם	לָתֵת	עַמּוֹ	אֶת־
And went out	bread	to them	to give	His people	←

וּשְׁתֵּי	שָׁמָּה	הָיְתָה־	אֲשֶׁר	הַמָּקוֹם	מִן־
and the two of	toward there	she was	which	the place	from

כלֹּתֶיהָ	עִמָּהּ	וַתֵּלַכְנָה	בַּדֶּרֶךְ	לָשׁוּב	אֶל־
her daughters-in-law	with her	and they walked	on the road	to return	to

אֶרֶץ	יְהוּדָה:	וַתֹּאמֶר	נָעֳמִי	לִשְׁתֵּי	כַלֹּתֶיהָ
the land of	Judah	And said	Naomi	to the two of	her daughters-in-law

לֵכְנָה	שֹׁבְנָה	אִשָּׁה	לְבֵית	אִמָּהּ	יַעַשׂ
walk	return	a woman	to the house of	her mother	may do

יְהוָה	עִמָּכֶם	חֶסֶד	כַּאֲשֶׁר	עֲשִׂיתֶם	עִם־
the LORD	with you	steadfast love	as	you did	with

הַמֵּתִים	וְעִמָּדִי	יִתֵּן	יְהֹוָה	לָכֶם	וּמְצֶאןָ
the dead men	and with me	May give	the LORD	to you	and may you find

מְנוּחָה	אִשָּׁה	בֵּית	אִישָׁהּ	וַתִּשַּׁק	לָהֶן
rest	a woman	the house of	her husband	and she kissed	(to) them

וַתִּשֶּׂאנָה	קוֹלָן	וַתִּבְכֶּינָה	וַתֹּאמַרְנָה	לָהּ	כִּי־
and they lifted	their voices	and wept	And they said	to her	that

אִתָּךְ	נָשׁוּב	לְעַמֵּךְ	וַתֹּאמֶר	נָעֳמִי	שֹׁבְנָה
with you	we will return	to your people	And said	Naomi	return

Ruth 1:11-12

בְּנֹתַי	לָמָּה	תֵלַכְנָה	עִמִּי	הַעוֹד־	לִי
my daughters	why	will you walk	with me	are there yet	to me

בָּנִים	בְּמֵעַי	וְהָיוּ	לָכֶם	לַאֲנָשִׁים:	שֹׁבְנָה
sons	in my womb	and they will be	to you	for husbands?	Return

בְּנֹתַי	לֵכְןָ	כִּי	זָקַנְתִּי	מִהְיוֹת	לְאִישׁ
my daughters	walk	because	I am old	to become	for a husband

כִּי	אָמַרְתִּי	יֶשׁ־	לִי	תִקְוָה	גַּם
if	I said	there is	to me	hope	even

Ruth 1:12-13

הָיִיתִי	הַלַּיְלָה	לְאִישׁ	וְגַם	יָלַדְתִּי	בָּנִים:
I was	tonight	for a husband	and even	I gave birth to	sons

הֲלָהֵן	תְּשַׂבֵּרְנָה	עַד	אֲשֶׁר	יִגְדָּלוּ	הֲלָהֵן
would therefore	you wait	until	which	they grew	would therefore

תֵּעָגֵנָה	לְבִלְתִּי	הֱיוֹת	לְאִישׁ	אַל	בְּנֹתַי
you refrain	to not	become	for a husband	do not	my daughters

כִּי-	מַר-	לִי	מְאֹד	מִכֶּם	כִּי-
because	bitter	to me	very	from you	because

קוֹלָן	וַתִּשֶּׂנָה	יְהוָה:	יַד־	בִי	יָצְאָה
their voices	And lifted up	the LORD	the hand of	on me	went out

וְרוּת	לַחֲמוֹתָה	עָרְפָּה	וַתִּשַּׁק	עוֹד	וַתִּבְכֶּינָה
and Ruth	(to) her mother-in-law	Orpah	and kissed	again	and wept

יְבִמְתֵּךְ	שָׁבָה	הִנֵּה	וַתֹּאמֶר	בָּהּ:	דָּבְקָה
your sister-in-law	returned	behold	And she said	with her	clung

אַחֲרֵי	שׁוּבִי	אֱלֹהֶיהָ	וְאֶל־	עַמָּהּ	אֶל־
after	return	her gods	and to	her people	to

Ruth 1:15-17

בִ֔י	תִּפְגְּעִי־	אַל־	רוּת	וַתֹּ֣אמֶר	יְבִמְתֵּ֔ךְ:
with me	entreat	do not	Ruth	And said	your sister-in-law

אֲשֶׁ֨ר	אֶל־	כִּ֠י	מֵאַחֲרָ֑יִךְ	לָשׁ֣וּב	לְעָזְבֵ֖ךְ
which	toward	because	from after you	to return	to leave you

עַמֵּ֣ךְ	אָלִ֔ין	תָּלִ֙ינִי֙	וּבַאֲשֶׁ֤ר	אֵלֵ֗ךְ	תֵּלְכִ֜י
your people	I will lodge	you lodge	and in which	I will walk	you will walk

אָמ֔וּת	תָּמ֙וּתִי֙	בַּאֲשֶׁ֤ר	אֱלֹהָֽי׃	וֵאלֹהַ֖יִךְ	עַמִּ֣י
I will die	you die	in which	my God	and your God	my people

Ruth 1:17-19

וְשָׁם	אֶקָּבֵר	כֹּה	יַעֲשֶׂה	יְהוָֹה	לִי
and there	I will be buried	thus	may do	the LORD	to me

וְכֹה	יֹסִיף	כִּי	הַמָּוֶת	יַפְרִיד	בֵּינִי
and thus	again	because	the death	will separate	between me

וּבֵינֵךְ:	וַתֵּרֶא	כִּי־	מִתְאַמֶּצֶת	הִיא	לָלֶכֶת
and between you	And she saw	that	determined, courageous	she	to walk

אִתָּה	וַתֶּחְדַּל	לְדַבֵּר	אֵלֶיהָ:	וַתֵּלַכְנָה	שְׁתֵּיהֶם
with her	and she ceased	to speak	to her	And walked	the two of them

כְּבֹאֲנָה	וַיְהִי	לֶחֶם	בֵּית	בֹּאֲנָה	עַד־
as they came	and it was	bread	house of	came	until

עֲלֵיהֶן	הָעִיר	כָּל־	וַתֵּהֹם	לֶחֶם	בֵּית
on them	the city	all	and made noise	bread	house of

אַל־	אֲלֵיהֶן	וַתֹּאמֶר	נָעֳמִי:	הֲזֹאת	וַתֹּאמַרְנָה
do not	to them	And she said	Naomi	this	and they said

מָרָא	לִי	קְרֶאןָ	נָעֳמִי	לִי	תִּקְרֶאנָה
Mara, bitter	me	call	Naomi	me	you will call

Ruth 1:20-21

אֲנִי	מְאֹד:	לִי	שַׁדַּי	הֵמַר	כִּי־
I	very	for me	the Almighty	made bitter	because

לָמָּה	יְהוָה	הֱשִׁיבַנִי	וְרֵיקָם	הָלַכְתִּי	מְלֵאָה
why	the LORD	returned me	and empty	I walked	filled

בִי	עָנָה	וַיהוָה	נָעֳמִי	לִי	תִקְרֶאנָה
against me	testified	and the LORD	Naomi	to me	you will call

וְרוּת	נָעֳמִי	וַתָּשָׁב	לִי:	הֵרַע	וְשַׁדַּי
and Ruth	Naomi	And returned	to me	caused affliction	and the Almighty

הַמּוֹאֲבִיָּה	כַּלָּתָהּ	עִמָּהּ	הַשָּׁבָה	מִשְּׂדֵי	מוֹאָב
the Moabitess	her daughter-in-law	with her	the one who returned	from the fields of	Moab

וְהֵמָּה	בָּאוּ	בֵּית	לֶחֶם	בִּתְחִלַּת	קְצִיר
and they	came	house of	bread	in the beginning of	harvesting of

שְׂעֹרִים:	וּלְנָעֳמִי	מוֹדָע	לְאִישָׁהּ	אִישׁ	גִּבּוֹר
barley	And to Naomi	someone known	to her husband	a man	strong

חַיִל	מִמִּשְׁפַּחַת	אֱלִימֶלֶךְ	וּשְׁמוֹ	בֹּעַז:	וַתֹּאמֶר
valiant	from the family of	Elimelech	and his name	Boaz	And said

Ruth 2:2-3 22

נָּא	אֵלְכָה־	נָעֳמִי	אֶל־	הַמּוֹאֲבִיָּה	רוּת
please	I will go	Naomi	to	the Moabitess	Ruth

אֶמְצָא־	אֲשֶׁר	אַחַר	בַשִׁבֳּלִים	וַאֲלַקֳטָה	הַשָּׂדֶה
I will find	which	after	in the ears of grain	and I will glean	the field

בִתִּי:	לְכִי	לָהּ	וַתֹּאמֶר	בְּעֵינָיו	חֵן
my daughter	go	to her	and said	in his eyes	grace

הַקֹּצְרִים	אַחֲרֵי	בַשָּׂדֶה	וַתְּלַקֵּט	וַתָּבוֹא	וַתֵּלֶךְ
the reapers	after	in the field	and gleaned	and came	and went

אֲשֶׁר	לְבֹעַז	הַשָּׂדֶה	חֶלְקַת	מִקְרֶהָ	וַיִּקֶר
which	(belonging) to Boaz	the field	a portion of ground of	her happening	and happened

מִבֵּית	בָּא	בֹּעַז	וְהִנֵּה-	אֱלִימֶלֶךְ:	מִמִּשְׁפַּחַת
from the house of	came	Boaz	And behold	Elimelech	from the family of

וַיֹּאמְרוּ	עִמָּכֶם	יְהוָה	לַקּוֹצְרִים	וַיֹּאמֶר	לֶחֶם
and they said	with you	the LORD	to the reapers	and said	bread

לְנַעֲרוֹ	בֹּעַז	וַיֹּאמֶר	יְהוָה:	יְבָרֶכְךָ	לוֹ
to his young man	Boaz	and said	the LORD	may bless you	to him

הַזֹּאת:	הַנַּעֲרָה	לְמִי	הַקּוֹצְרִים	עַל־	הַנִּצָּב
the this	the young woman	to whom	the reapers	with	stationed

וַיֹּאמַר	הַקּוֹצְרִים	עַל־	הַנִּצָּב	הַנַּעַר	וַיַּעַן
and said	the reapers	with	stationed	the young man	And replied

נָעֳמִי	עִם־	הַשָּׁבָה	הִיא	מוֹאֲבִיָּה	נַעֲרָה
Naomi	with	the one who returned	she	Moabitish	a young woman

וְאָסַפְתִּי	נָא	אֲלַקֳטָה־	וַתֹּאמֶר	מוֹאָב	מִשְּׂדֵה
and I will gather	please	I will glean	And she said	Moab	from the fields of

Ruth 2:7-8

בָּעֳמָרִים	אַחֲרֵי	הַקּוֹצְרִים	וַתָּבוֹא	וַתַּעֲמוֹד	מֵאָז
in the sheaves	after	the reapers	and she came	and she stood	from then

הַבֹּקֶר	וְעַד-	עַתָּה	זֶה	שִׁבְתָּהּ	הַבַּיִת
the morning	and until	now	this	she remained	in the house

מְעָט:	וַיֹּאמֶר	בֹּעַז	אֶל-	רוּת	הֲלוֹא
a little	and said	Boaz	to	Ruth	will not?

שָׁמַעַתְּ	בִּתִּי	אַל-	תֵּלְכִי	לִלְקֹט	בְּשָׂדֶה
you hear	my daughter	do not	go	to glean	in a field

Ruth 2:8-9

וְכֹה	מִזֶּה	תַעֲבוּרִי	לֹא	וְגַם	אַחֵר
and thus	from this	cross over	do not	and also	another

אֲשֶׁר־	בְּשָׂדֶה	עֵינַיִךְ	נַעֲרֹתָי:	עִם־	תִדְבָּקִין
which	on the field	Your eyes	my young women	with	you will keep close

אֶת־	צִוִּיתִי	הֲלוֹא	אַחֲרֵיהֶן	וְהָלַכְתְּ	יִקְצֹרוּן
←	I commanded	have not?	after them	and you go	they reap

אֶל־	וְהָלַכְתְּ	וְצָמִת	נָגְעֵךְ	לְבִלְתִּי	הַנְּעָרִים
to	and you will go	and you will thirst	touch you	to not	the young men

הַכֵּלִים	וְשָׁתִית	מֵאֲשֶׁר	יִשְׁאֲבוּן	הַנְּעָרִים:	וַתִּפֹּל
the vessels	and you will drink	from which	will draw	the young men	And she fell

עַל־	פָּנֶיהָ	וַתִּשְׁתַּחוּ	אַרְצָה	וַתֹּאמֶר	אֵלָיו
on	her face	and bowed herself down	toward the ground	and she said	to him

מַדּוּעַ	מָצָאתִי	חֵן	בְּעֵינֶיךָ	לְהַכִּירֵנִי	וְאָנֹכִי
why?	I found	grace	in your eyes	to cause you to take notice of me	and I

נָכְרִיָּה:	וַיַּעַן	בֹּעַז	וַיֹּאמֶר	לָהּ	הֻגֵּד
a foreigner	And replied	Boaz	and he said	to her	to report

אֶת־	עָשִׂית	אֲשֶׁר־	כֹּל	לִי	הֻגַּד
with	you did	which	all	to me	it has been reported

אָבִיךְ	וַתַּעַזְבִי	אִישֵׁךְ	מוֹת	אַחֲרֵי	חֲמוֹתֵךְ
your father	and you left	your husband	the death of	after	your mother-in-law

עַם	אֶל־	וַתֵּלְכִי	מוֹלַדְתֵּךְ	וְאֶרֶץ	וְאִמֵּךְ
a people	to	and you came	your birth	and the land of	and your mother

יְשַׁלֵּם	שִׁלְשׁוֹם:	תְּמוֹל	יָדַעַתְּ	לֹא־	אֲשֶׁר
Will recompense	the day before yesterday	before	you knew	not	which

Ruth 2:12-13

מֵעִם	שְׁלֵמָה	מַשְׂכֻּרְתֵּךְ	וּתְהִי	פָּעֳלֵךְ	יְהוָה
from with	complete	your wages	and will be	your work	the LORD

לַחְסוֹת	בָּאת	אֲשֶׁר־	יִשְׂרָאֵל	אֱלֹהֵי	יְהוָה
to seek refuge	you came	which	Israel	the God of	the LORD

בְּעֵינֶיךָ	חֵן	אֶמְצָא־	וַתֹּאמֶר	כְּנָפָיו׃	תַּחַת־
in your eyes	grace	may I find	And she said	his wings	under

עַל־	דִּבַּרְתָּ	וְכִי	נִחַמְתָּנִי	כִּי	אֲדֹנִי
on	you spoke	and because	you comforted me	because	my lord

כְּאַחַת	אֶהְיֶה	לֹא	וְאָנֹכִי	שִׁפְחָתֶךָ	לֵב
like one of	will be	not	and I	your maidservant	the heart of

הָאֹכֶל	לְעֵת	בֹעַז	לָה	וַיֹּאמֶר	שִׁפְחֹתֶיךָ:
the food	for the time of	Boaz	to her	And said	your maidservants

וְטָבַלְתְּ	הַלֶּחֶם	מִן־	וְאָכַלְתְּ	הֲלֹם	גֹּשִׁי
and you will dip	the bread	from	and you will eat	here	draw near

וַיִּצְבָּט־	הַקּוֹצְרִים	מִצַּד	וַתֵּשֶׁב	בַּחֹמֶץ	פִּתֵּךְ
and he served	the reapers	at the side of	and she sat	in the vinegar	your piece

לָהּ	קָלִי	וַתֹּאכַל	וַתִּשְׂבַּע	וַתֹּתַר:	וַתָּקָם
to her	roasted grain	and she ate	and she was satisfied	and she caused some to be left	And she arose

לְלַקֵּט	וַיְצַו	בֹּעַז	אֶת־	נְעָרָיו	לֵאמֹר
to glean	and commanded	Boaz	←	his young men	saying

גַּם	בֵּין	הָעֳמָרִים	תְּלַקֵּט	וְלֹא	תַכְלִימוּהָ:
also	between	the sheaves	she will glean	and do not	humiliate her

וְגַם	שֹׁל־	תָּשֹׁלּוּ	לָהּ	מִן־	הַצְּבָתִים
And also	to pull	you will pull	for her	from	the sheaves

וַתְּלַקֵּט	בָהּ:	תִגְעֲרוּ־	וְלֹא	וְלִקְּטָה	וַעֲזַבְתֶּם
And she gleaned	(in) her	you will rebuke	and do not	and she will glean	and you will leave

אֲשֶׁר־	אֵת	וַתַּחְבֹּט	הָעֶרֶב	עַד־	בַּשָּׂדֶה
which	←	and she beat out	the evening	until	in the field

וַתָּבוֹא	וַתִּשָּׂא	שְׂעֹרִים:	כְּאֵיפָה	וַיְהִי	לִקֵּטָה
and she walked	And she carried	barley	about an ephah of	and it was	she gleaned

לִקֵּטָה	אֲשֶׁר־	אֵת	חֲמוֹתָהּ	וַתֵּרֶא	הָעִיר
she gleaned	which	←	her mother-in-law	and saw	the city

Ruth 2:18-19

הוֹתִרָה	אֲשֶׁר־	אֵת	לָהּ	וַתִּתֶּן־	וַתּוֹצֵא
remained	which	←	to her	and she gave	and she brought out

לִקֵּטְתְּ	אֵיפֹה	חֲמוֹתָהּ	לָהּ	וַתֹּאמֶר	מִשָּׂבְעָהּ:
you gleaned	where?	her mother-in-law	to her	And said	from her satisfaction

בָּרוּךְ	מַכִּירֵךְ	יְהִי	עָשִׂית	וְאָנָה	הַיּוֹם
blessed	the one who took notice of you	may be	you did	and where?	today

עִמּוֹ	עָשְׂתָה	אֲשֶׁר־	אֵת	לַחֲמוֹתָהּ	וַתַּגֵּד
with him	she did	which	←	to her mother-in-law	and she made known

Ruth 2:19-20   34

עִמּוֹ	עָשִׂיתִי	אֲשֶׁר	הָאִישׁ	שֵׁם	וַתֹּאמֶר
with him	I did	which	the man	the name of	and she said

בָּרוּךְ	לְכַלָּתָהּ	נָעֳמִי	וַתֹּאמֶר	בֹּעַז:	הַיּוֹם
blessed	to her daughter-in-law	Naomi	And said	Boaz	today

חַסְדּוֹ	עָזַב	לֹא־	אֲשֶׁר	לַיהוָה	הוּא
his steadfast love	leave	did not	which	to the LORD	he

לָהּ	וַתֹּאמֶר	הַמֵּתִים	וְאֶת־	הַחַיִּים	אֶת־
to her	and said	the dead	and with	the living	with

Ruth 2:20-21

הוּא:	מְגֹאֲלֵנוּ	הָאִישׁ	לָנוּ	קָרוֹב	נָעֳמִי
he	our kinsman redeemer	the man	to us	near	Naomi

אָמַר	כִּי־	גַם	הַמּוֹאֲבִיָּה	רוּת	וַתֹּאמֶר
he said	because	also	the Moabitess	Ruth	And said

תִּדְבָּקִין	לִי	אֲשֶׁר־	הַנְּעָרִים	עִם־	אֵלַי
you will keep close	to me	which	the young men	with	to me

הַקָּצִיר	כָּל־	אֵת	כִּלּוּ	אִם־	עַד
the harvest	all	←	they finished	if	until

Ruth 2:21-23

אֲשֶׁר־	לִי:	וַתֹּאמֶר	נָעֳמִי	אֶל־	רוּת
which	to me	And said	Naomi	to	Ruth

כַּלָּתָהּ	טוֹב	בִּתִּי	כִּי	תֵצְאִי	עִם־
her daughter-in-law	good	my daughter	because	you will go out	with

נַעֲרוֹתָיו	וְלֹא	יִפְגְּעוּ־	בָךְ	בְּשָׂדֶה	אַחֵר:
his young women	and not	they will meet	with you	in a field	another

וַתִּדְבַּק	בְּנַעֲרוֹת	בֹּעַז	לְלַקֵּט	עַד־	כְּלוֹת
And she kept close	with the young women of	Boaz	to glean	until	to be finished

קְצִיר־	הַשְּׂעֹרִים	וּקְצִיר	הַחִטִּים	וַתֵּשֶׁב	אֶת־
the harvest of	the barley	and the harvest of	the wheat	and she dwelt	with

חֲמוֹתָהּ:	וַתֹּאמֶר	לָהּ	נָעֳמִי	חֲמוֹתָהּ	בִּתִּי
her mother-in-law	And said	to her	Naomi	her mother-in-law	my daughter

הֲלֹא	אֲבַקֶּשׁ־	לָךְ	מָנוֹחַ	אֲשֶׁר	יִיטַב־
not?	I will seek	for you	rest	which	will be good

לָךְ:	וְעַתָּה	הֲלֹא	בֹעַז	מֹדַעְתָּנוּ	אֲשֶׁר
for you	And now	not?	Boaz	someone known to us	which

Ruth 3:2-3:3

זֹרֶה	הוּא	הִנֵּה־	נַעֲרוֹתָיו	אֶת־	הָיִית
is winnowing	he	behold	his young women	with ·	you were

וָסַכְתְּ	וְרָחַצְתְּ	הַלָּיְלָה:	הַשְּׂעֹרִים	גֹּרֶן	אֶת־
and you will anoint	You will bathe	tonight	the barley	the threshing floor of	←

אַל־	הַגֹּרֶן	וְיָרַדְתְּ	עָלַיִךְ	שִׂמְלֹתַיִךְ	וְשַׂמְתְּ
do not	the threshing floor	and you will go down	on you	your cloak	and you will put

וְלִשְׁתּוֹת:	לֶאֱכֹל	כַּלֹּתוֹ	עַד	לָאִישׁ	תּוֹדְעִי
and to drink	to eat	his being finished	until	to the man	be known

אֲשֶׁר	הַמָּקוֹם	אֶת־	וְיָדַעַתְּ	בְּשָׁכְבוֹ	וִיהִי
which	the place	←	and you will know	in his lying down	Shall be

וְשָׁכָבְתְּ	מַרְגְּלֹתָיו	וְגִלִּית	וּבָאת	שָׁם	יִשְׁכַּב־
and you will lie down	his feet	and uncover	and you will go	there	he will lie down

תַּעֲשִׂין:	אֲשֶׁר	אֵת	לָךְ	יַגִּיד	וְהוּא
you will do	which	←	to you	will tell	and he

אֵלָי	תֹּאמְרִי	אֲשֶׁר־	כֹּל	אֵלֶיהָ	וַתֹּאמֶר
to me	you will say	which	all	to her	And she said

Ruth 3:5-8

אֲשֶׁר-	כְּכֹל	וַתַּעַשׂ	הַגֹּרֶן	וַתֵּרֶד	אֶעֱשֶׂה:
which	like all	and she did	the threshing floor	And she went down	I will do

וַיִּיטַב	וַיֵּשְׁתְּ	בֹּעַז	וַיֹּאכַל	חֲמוֹתָהּ:	צִוַּתָּה
and was joyful	and drank	Boaz	And ate	her mother-in-law	commanded her

וַתָּבֹא	הָעֲרֵמָה	בִּקְצֵה	לִשְׁכַּב	וַיָּבֹא	לִבּוֹ
and she came	the heaps of grain	at the edge of	to lie down	and came	his heart

בַּחֲצִי	וַיְהִי	וַתִּשְׁכָּב:	מַרְגְּלֹתָיו	וַתְּגַל	בַּלָּט
in the half of	and it was	and she lay down	his feet	and uncovered	secretly

הַלַּיְלָה	וַיֶּחֱרַד	הָאִישׁ	וַיִּלָּפֵת	וְהִנֵּה	אִשָּׁה
the night	and was frightened	the man	and he turned	and behold!	a woman

שֹׁכֶבֶת	מַרְגְּלֹתָיו:	וַיֹּאמֶר	מִי־	אָתְּ	וַתֹּאמֶר
lay	his feet	And he said	who	you	and she said

אָנֹכִי	רוּת	אֲמָתֶךָ	וּפָרַשְׂתָּ	כְנָפֶךָ	עַל־
I	Ruth	your maidservant	and spread out	your wing	over

אֲמָתְךָ	כִּי	גֹאֵל	אָתָּה:	וַיֹּאמֶר	בְּרוּכָה
your maidservant	because	a kinsman redeemer	you	and he said	blessed

הָאַחֲרוֹן	חַסְדֵּךְ	הֵיטַבְתְּ	בִּתִּי	לַיהוָה	אַתְּ
the last	your steadfast love	you have made good, right	my daughter	to the LORD	you

הַבַּחוּרִים	אַחֲרֵי	לֶכֶת	לְבִלְתִּי־	הָרִאשׁוֹן	מִן־
the young men	after	go	to not	the first	from

בִּתִּי	וְעַתָּה	עָשִׁיר:	וְאִם־	דַּל	אִם־
my daughter	And you	rich	and if	poor	if

אֶעֱשֶׂה־	תֹּאמְרִי	אֲשֶׁר־	כֹּל	תִּירְאִי	אַל־
I will do	you will say	which	all	fear	do not

43 Ruth 3:11-13

עַמִּי	שַׁעַר	כָּל־	יוֹדֵעַ	כִּי	לָךְ
my people	the gate of	all	is knowing	because	for you

כִּי	וְעַתָּה	אָתְּ:	חַיִל	אֵשֶׁת	כִּי
because	And now	you	valor	a woman of	that

יֵשׁ	וְגַם	אָנֹכִי	גֹאֵל	כִּי	אָמְנָם
there is	and also	I	a kinsman redeemer	that	truly

וְהָיָה	הַלַּיְלָה	לִינִי	מִמֶּנִּי:	קָרוֹב	גֹאֵל
and it will be	the night	lodge	from me	near	a kinsman redeemer

וְאִם־	יִגְאָל	טוֹב	יִגְאָלֵךְ	אִם־	בַּבֹּקֶר
and if	he will redeem	good	he will redeem you	if	in the morning

חַי־	אָנֹכִי	וּגְאַלְתִּיךְ	לְגָאֳלֵךְ	יַחְפֹּץ	לֹא
living	I	and will redeem you	to redeem you	he will desire	not

מַרְגְּלוֹתָיו	וַתִּשְׁכַּב	הַבֹּקֶר:	עַד־	שִׁכְבִי	יְהוָה
his feet	and she lay	the morning	until	lie down	the LORD

אִישׁ	יַכִּיר	בְּטֶרֶם	וַתָּקָם	הַבֹּקֶר	עַד־
a man	will recognize	before	and she rose	the morning	until

אֶת־	רֵעֵהוּ	וַיֹּאמֶר	אַל־	יִוָּדַע	כִּי־
←	his neighbor	and he said	not	will be known	that

בָּאָה	הָאִשָּׁה	הַגֹּרֶן:	וַיֹּאמֶר	הָבִי	הַמִּטְפַּחַת
came	a woman	the threshing floor	And he said	give	the cloak

אֲשֶׁר־	עָלַיִךְ	וְאֶחֳזִי־	בָהּ	וַתֹּאחֶז	בָּהּ
which	on you	and hold	(in) it	and she held	(in) it

וַיָּמָד	שֵׁשׁ־	שְׂעֹרִים	וַיָּשֶׁת	עָלֶיהָ	וַיָּבֹא
and he measured	six	barleys	and he set	on her	and she went

Ruth 3:15-17

מִי־	וַתֹּאמֶר	חֲמוֹתָהּ	אֶל־	וַתָּבוֹא	הָעִיר:
who?	and she said	her mother-in-law	to	And she came	the city

כָּל־	אֵת	לָהּ	וַתַּגֶּד־	בִּתִּי	אַתְּ
all	←	to her	and she told	my daughter	you

שֵׁשׁ־	וַתֹּאמֶר	הָאִישׁ:	לָהּ	עָשָׂה־	אֲשֶׁר
six	And she said	the man	to her	did	which

אָמַר	כִּי	לִי	נָתַן	הָאֵלֶּה	הַשְּׂעֹרִים
he said	because	to me	he gave	these	barleys

חֲמוֹתֵךְ:	אֶל־	רֵיקָם	תָּבוֹאִי	אַל־	אֵלַי
your mother-in-law	to	empty-handed	you will go	not	to me

תֵּדְעִין	אֲשֶׁר	עַד	בִּתִּי	שְׁבִי	וַתֹּאמֶר
you will know	which	until	my daughter	sit	And she said

יִשְׁקֹט	לֹא	כִּי	דָּבָר	יִפֹּל	אֵיךְ
will be inactive	not	because	a thing	will fall	how?

הַיּוֹם:	הַדָּבָר	כִּלָּה	אִם־	כִּי־	הָאִישׁ
today	the thing	he finished	if	because	the man

וְהִנֵּה	שָׁם	וַיֵּשֶׁב	הַשַּׁעַר	עָלָה	וּבֹעַז
and behold	there	and sat	the gate	went up	And Boaz

וַיֹּאמֶר	בֹּעַז	דִּבֶּר־	אֲשֶׁר	עֹבֵר	הַגֹּאֵל
and he said	Boaz	spoke	which	crossing over	the kinsman redeemer

וַיָּסַר	אַלְמֹנִי	פְּלֹנִי	פֹּה	שְׁבָה־	סוּרָה
and he turned aside	someone	a certain	there	sit	turn aside

הָעִיר	מִזְּקְנֵי	אֲנָשִׁים	עֲשָׂרָה	וַיִּקַּח	וַיֵּשֵׁב:
the city	from the elders of	men	ten	And he took	and sat

Ruth 4:2-4

לַגֹּאֵל	וַיֹּאמֶר	וַיֵּשֵׁבוּ׃	פֹּה	שְׁבוּ־	וַיֹּאמֶר
to the kinsman redeemer	And he said	and they sat	there	sit	and he said

מְכָרָה	לֶאֱלִימֶלֶךְ	לְאָחִינוּ	אֲשֶׁר	הַשָּׂדֶה	חֶלְקַת
sold	to Elimelech	to our brother	which	the field	a portion of ground of

אָמַרְתִּי	וַאֲנִי	מוֹאָב׃	מִשְּׂדֵה	הַשָּׁבָה	נָעֳמִי
said	And I	Moab	from the fields of	the one who returned	Naomi

הַיֹּשְׁבִים	נֶגֶד	קְנֵה	לֵאמֹר	אָזְנְךָ	אֶגְלֶה
the residents	before	buy	to say	your ear	I will uncover

Ruth 4:4-5

וְנֶגֶד	זִקְנֵי	עַמִּי	אִם־	תִּגְאַל	גְּאָל
and before	the elders of	my people	if	you will redeem	redeem

וְאִם־	לֹא	יִגְאַל	הַגִּידָה	לִּי	וְאֵדְעָה
and if	not	I will redeem	tell	to me	and I will know

כִּי	אֵין	זוּלָתְךָ	לִגְאוֹל	וְאָנֹכִי	אַחֲרֶיךָ
because	there is not	except you	to redeem	and I	after you

וַיֹּאמֶר	אָנֹכִי	אֶגְאָל:	וַיֹּאמֶר	בֹּעַז	בְּיוֹם־
and said	I	I will redeem	And said	Boaz	on the day

Ruth 4:5-6

קְנוֹתְךָ	הַשָּׂדֶה	מִיַּד	נָעֳמִי	וּמֵאֵת	רוּת
acquire	the field	from the hand of	Naomi	and with it	Ruth

הַמּוֹאֲבִיָּה	אֵשֶׁת־	הַמֵּת	קָנִיתָה	לְהָקִים	שֵׁם־
the Moabitess	wife of	the dead man	you will acquire	to establish	the name of

הַמֵּת	עַל־	נַחֲלָתוֹ:	וַיֹּאמֶר	הַגֹּאֵל	לֹא
the dead man	on	his inheritance	And said	the kinsman redeemer	not

אוּכַל	לִגְאָל־	לִי	פֶּן־	אַשְׁחִית	אֶת־
I will be able	to redeem	to me	lest	I will ruin	←

גָּאַלְתִּי	אֶת־	אַתָּה	לְךָ	גְּאַל־	נַחֲלָתִי
my right of redemption	←	you	to you	redeem	my inheritance

לְפָנִים	וְזֹאת	לִגְאֹל׃	אוּכַל	לֹא־	כִּי
to the faces	And this	to redeem	I will be able	not	because

לְקַיֵּם	הַתְּמוּרָה	וְעַל־	הַגְּאוּלָּה	עַל־	בְּיִשְׂרָאֵל
to establish	the substitution	and on	the redemption	on	in Israel

וְנָתַן	נַעֲלוֹ	אִישׁ	שָׁלַף	דָּבָר	כָּל־
and gave	his sandal	a man	drew off	thing	every

Ruth 4:7-9

הַגֹּאֵל	וַיֹּאמֶר	בְּיִשְׂרָאֵל:	הַתְּעוּדָה	וְזֹאת	לְרֵעֵהוּ
the kinsman redeemer	And said	in Israel	the testimony	and this	his neighbor

וַיֹּאמֶר	נַעֲלוֹ:	וַיִּשְׁלֹף	לָךְ	קְנֵה־	לְבֹעַז
And said	his sandal	and he drew off	to you	acquire	to Boaz

אַתֶּם	עֵדִים	הָעָם	וְכָל־	לַזְּקֵנִים	בֹּעַז
you	witnesses	the people	and all	to the elders	Boaz

אֲשֶׁר	כָּל־	אֶת־	קָנִיתִי	כִּי	הַיּוֹם
which	all	←	I acquired	that	today

וּמַחְלוֹן	לְכִלְיוֹן	אֲשֶׁר	כָּל־	וְאֵת	לְאֱלִימֶלֶךְ
and Machlon	to Chilion	which	all	and ←	to Elimelech

הַמֹּאֲבִיָּה	רוּת	אֶת־	וְגַם	נָעֳמִי:	מִיַּד
the Moabitess	Ruth	←	And also	Naomi	from the hand of

לְהָקִים	לְאִשָּׁה	לִי	קָנִיתִי	מַחְלוֹן	אֵשֶׁת
to establish	for a wife	to me	I acquired	Machlon	the wife of

יִכָּרֵת	וְלֹא־	נַחֲלָתוֹ	עַל־	הַמֵּת	שֵׁם־
will be cut off	and not	his inheritance	on	the dead man	the name of

Ruth 4:10-11

מְקוֹמוֹ	וּמִשַּׁעַר	אֶחָיו	מֵעִם	הַמֵּת	שֵׁם־
his place	and from with the gate of	his brothers	from with	the dead man	the name of

הָעָם	כָּל־	וַיֹּאמְרוּ	הַיּוֹם:	אַתֶּם	עֵדִים
the people	all	And said	today	you	witnesses

יְהוָה	יִתֵּן	עֵדִים	וְהַזְּקֵנִים	בַּשַּׁעַר	אֲשֶׁר־
the LORD	may give	witnesses	and the elders	in the gate	which

כְּרָחֵל	בֵּיתֶךָ	אֶל־	הַבָּאָה	הָאִשָּׁה	אֶת־
like Rachel	your house	to	the one who came	the woman	←

Ruth 4:11-12

בֵּית	אֶת־	שְׁתֵּיהֶם	בָּנוּ	אֲשֶׁר	וּכְלֵאָה
the house of	←	the two of them	built	which	and like Leah

שֵׁם	וּקְרָא־	בְּאֶפְרָתָה	חַיִל	וַעֲשֵׂה־	יִשְׂרָאֵל
a name	and proclaim	in Ephrathah	valiantly	and do (you)	Israel

פֶּרֶץ	כְּבֵית	בֵיתְךָ	וִיהִי	לָחֶם:	בְּבֵית
Perez	like the house of	your house	And may it be	bread	in the house of

הַזֶּרַע	מִן־	לִיהוּדָה	תָּמָר	יָלְדָה	אֲשֶׁר־
the seed	from	for Judah	Tamar	gave birth to	which

Ruth 4:12-14

אֲשֶׁר	יִתֵּן	יְהֹוָה	לְךָ	מִן־	הַנַּעֲרָה
which	will give	the LORD	to you	from	the young woman

הַזֹּאת:	וַיִּקַּח	בֹּעַז	אֶת־	רוּת	וַתְּהִי־
the this	And took	Boaz	←	Ruth	and she was

לוֹ	לְאִשָּׁה	וַיָּבֹא	אֵלֶיהָ	וַיִּתֵּן	יְהֹוָה
to him	for a wife	and he came	to her	and gave	the LORD

לָהּ	הֵרָיוֹן	וַתֵּלֶד	בֵּן:	וַתֹּאמַרְנָה	הַנָּשִׁים
to her	pregnancy	and she gave birth to	a son	And said	the women

Ruth 4:14-15

לֹא	אֲשֶׁר	יְהוָה	בָּרוּךְ	נָעֳמִי	אֶל־
not	which	the LORD	blessed	Naomi	to

שְׁמוֹ	וְיִקָּרֵא	הַיּוֹם	גֹּאֵל	לָךְ	הִשְׁבִּית
his name	and will be proclaimed	today	a kinsman redeemer	to you	ceased

וּלְכַלְכֵּל	נֶפֶשׁ	לְמֵשִׁיב	לָךְ	וְהָיָה	בְּיִשְׂרָאֵל:
and to sustain	soul/life	for restoring	to you	And he will be	in Israel

אֲהֵבַתֶךְ	אֲשֶׁר־	כַּלָּתֵךְ	כִּי	שֵׁיבָתֵךְ	אֶת־
loved you	which	your daughter-in-law	because	your old age	←

Ruth 4:15-17

מִשִּׁבְעָה	לָךְ	טוֹבָה	הִיא	אֲשֶׁר־	יְלָדַתּוּ
from seven	to you	good	she	which	gave birth to him

וַתְּשִׁתֵהוּ	הַיֶּלֶד	אֶת־	נָעֳמִי	וַתִּקַּח	בָּנִים:
and set him	the child	←	Naomi	And took	sons

לוֹ	וַתִּקְרֶאנָה	לֵאמֶנֶת:	לוֹ	וַתְּהִי־	בְּחֵיקָה
to him	And proclaimed	a supportive caregiver	to him	and she was	on her bosom

לְנָעֳמִי	בֵּן	יֻלַּד־	לֵאמֹר	שֵׁם	הַשְּׁכֵנוֹת
to Naomi	a son	born	saying	a name	the neighbors

וַתִּקְרֶאנָה	שְׁמוֹ	עוֹבֵד	הוּא	אֲבִי־	יִשָׁי
and they called	his name	Obed	he	father of	Jesse

אֲבִי	דָּוִד:	וְאֵלֶּה	תּוֹלְדוֹת	פֶּרֶץ	פֶּרֶץ
father of	David	And these	the generations of	Perez	Perez

הוֹלִיד	אֶת־	חֶצְרוֹן:	וְחֶצְרוֹן	הוֹלִיד	אֶת־
fathered	←	Hezron	And Hezron	fathered	←

רָם	וְרָם	הוֹלִיד	אֶת־	עַמִּינָדָב:	וְעַמִּינָדָב
Ram	and Ram	fathered	←	Amminadab	And Amminadab

Ruth 4:20-22

אֶת־	הוֹלִיד	וְנַחְשׁוֹן	נַחְשׁוֹן	אֶת־	הוֹלִיד
←	fathered	and Nahshon	Nahshon	←	fathered

וּבֹעַז	בֹּעַז	אֶת־	הוֹלִיד	וְשַׂלְמוֹן	שַׂלְמָה:
and Boaz	Boaz	←	fathered	And Salmon	Salmon

אֶת־	הוֹלִיד	וְעֹבֵד	עוֹבֵד:	אֶת־	הוֹלִיד
←	fathered	And Obed	Obed	←	fathered

דָּוִד:	אֶת־	הוֹלִיד	וְיִשַׁי	יִשַׁי
David	←	fathered	and Jesse	Jesse

HEBREW VOWEL POINTS

Vowel Point	Pronunciation
אֻ	oo
אְ	pronounce consonant
אוֹי	oi
אַי	aye

Vowel Point	Pronunciation
אָ	ah
אֳ	oh
אַ	ah
אֲ	ah
אִ	ee
אֵ	ay
אֱ	eh
אֶ	eh
אוֹ	oh
אֹ	oh
אוּ	oo

ah = a as in mama
oh = o as in go
ee = ee as in sheep
eh = e as in egg
ay = ay as in way
oo = oo as in zoo

HEBREW LETTERS

Pronunciation	Script	Block	Letter	Pronunciation	Script	Block	Letter
L as in land	ℓ	ל	ל	silent letter	lc	X	א
M as in mom	PN	םא	מם	B as in boy V as in very	בב	בב	בּ ב
N as in nut	| |	ןנ	נן	G as in goat	c	ג	ג
S as in sun	0	ס	ס	D as in day	ף	ד	ד
silent letter	४	ע	ע	H as in hen	ה	ה	ה
P as in pop F as in fish	ℓℓℓ	פףף	פפף	V as in very	|	ו	ו
TS as in hats	४ 3	צץ	צץ	Z as in zoo	ƽ	ז	ז
K as in kite	ק	ק	ק	ch as in Bach	ח	ח	ח
R as in red	ר	ר	ר	T as in tart	G	ט	ט
SH as in shine S as in sun	'e e'	שׁשׁ	שׁשׂ	Y as in yes	ı	י	י
T as in tart	ת	ת	ת	K as in kite ch as in Bach	ככך	ככך	כּכך

PAGE NOTES

Page 8, Ruth 1:1

To judge: construct infinitive. Remember that the direct object marker precedes definite direct objects, so we can see that the judges here are judging, not being judged.

The house of bread: "Bethlehem" is the transliteration of this Hebrew place name.

And the two of his sons: both of them

Page 12, Ruth 1:8

And they walked: Feminine plural forms are not common in Biblical Hebrew, but you get plenty of practice with them in Ruth.

a woman: each woman

חֶסֶד : Watch this word. Many consider it the central theme of the book. חֶסֶד incorporates steadfastness, love, and covenant devotion.

May do: The Hebrew imperfect tense verbs, like this one, describe incomplete actions. Possible translations of this word, depending on its context, include "he will do," "may he do," "he usually does," "he would do," and "he might do." Here, we have suggested "May do," representing a hope of Naomi's rather than a conjecture (He might...) or prophetic promise (He will...).

Page 13, Ruth 1:9

and she kissed (to) them: Hebrew and English have different ideas about when prepositions are needed. "To" is there in Hebrew, but we do not need it in an English translation.

Page 14, Ruth 1:11-12

Are there yet: Here is the interrogative hey prefix, indicating a question.

Will you walk/Walk: Commands are formed by dropping the tav prefix of the second person imperfect tense conjugation. תֵלַכְנָה is the feminine, plural, second person, imperfect tense conjugation. The feminine plural command *to walk*, לֵכְנָה, appeared in verse 1:8. Here it is again, but spelled differently: לֵכְן

because: כִּי means "that" or "because." In other words, it joins a subordinate clause to other words in a sentence and sometimes indicates a causal relationship. We have many words in English that do things like that (e.g. since, although, if) and they will come in handy for translating כִּי. Here, "if" makes better sense of the second כִּי than "because," so that 1:12 reads "*If* I said there is to me hope..."

Page 15, Ruth 1:13

bitter to me very from you: Here we see the preposition מ used to make a comparison of how bitter it is for Naomi compared to her daughters-in-law.

Page 19, Ruth 1:19

came house of bread: An example of a spot where English calls for a preposition but Hebrew gets along without one. We would say, "came *to* Bethlehem."

and they said: Notice that the feminine verb ending indicates this is specifically the women who are asking, "Is this Naomi?"

Mara, bitter: "Naomi" is derived from the word נֹעַם, meaning "delightful." When Naomi says, "Call me bitter" she is not admitting to resentment against Providence in Hebrew, as she might be in English with those words. The Hebrew root connotes (besides flavor) unpleasantness, intensity, distress, and sadness.

Naomi is contrasting her name with her circumstances, but not implying indignation or blame. Our English word can be used the Hebrew way or have negative overtones of sinful, lasting resentment. Here is an example of the value of studying original words in Biblical context, rather than in an English dictionary.

the two of them: Yup, that's a masculine ending to refer to Naomi and Ruth. It is used again at Ruth 4:11 to refer to Rachel and Leah. Go figure. This word is used with the expected feminine ending at 1 Samuel 25:43 to refer to David's wives.

Ruth Chapter One

Several examples of chiastic structure can be identified in the book of Ruth. The events of Chapter One form the inverted parallelism loved by Biblical writers.

A famine
 B move from Bethlehem to Moab
  C Naomi's name ("pleasant")
   D leave for Bethlehem
    E Naomi's speech
     F Naomi kisses Orpah and Ruth goodbye
      G all weep
       H young women wish to stay with Naomi
        I no hope of sons or husbands
       H´ Naomi wishes young women to return
      G´ all weep
     F´ Orpah kisses Naomi goodbye
    E´ Ruth's speech
   D´ arrive in Bethlehem
  C´ Naomi's name ("bitter")
 B´ move from Moab to Bethlehem
A´ barley harvest

The central line of a chiasmus is often its focus. Notice that the pivot point (**I**: no hope of sons or husbands) is indeed the crux of the beginning of the story and sets the stage for the unexpectedly wonderful resolution.

Page 25, Ruth 2:7

she remained in the house a little: Translations agree that Ruth was working hard that day, but vary a bit in the rendering of this Hebrew sentence:

except for a short rest in the shelter (NIV)
[she] hath not gone home for one moment (Douay-Rheims, an English translation of the Latin Vulgate)
except that she tarried a little in the house (KJV)
She did not rest a bit in the field (NETS, an English translation of the Septuagint)

Page 27, Ruth 2:10

to cause you to take notice of me, לְהַכִּירֵנִי: Here is the root נכר, which means to recognize. But it is in the causative action hifil stem, so something causes recognition. Here the root appears as a construct infinitive with a lamed preposition prefix: *to cause recognition*. And there is a first person pronoun suffix as well, referring to Ruth, the speaker: *to cause recognition of me*.

Page 27, Ruth 2:11

to report, הֻגַּד: An absolute infinitive in the hofal verb stem. The next word (on page 28) is the same root in the hofal verb stem, but conjugated in the masculine, singular, third person. The root is נגד, meaning "to tell." Hofal verbs are causative action, passive voice, so Boaz is saying somebody caused it to be told to him, or in better English, "I have been told…" The absolute infinitive before the normally conjugated verb indicates emphasis. So Boaz has been told with certainty, or told fully.

before the day before yesterday: Not literally the day before yesterday. This is a Hebrew idiom for which we might say "hitherto" or "formerly." This idiom is used about twenty-five times in the Bible. See it in action by looking up שִׁלְשׁוֹם in a concordance and tracing the references.

Page 29, Ruth 2:13
you comforted me: Piel stem (intensive action, active voice) with first person pronoun ending.

Page 30, Ruth 2:13
And I not will be: Here is an example of the imperfect tense meaning uncompleted rather than future action. Ruth is not making a prediction or a promise about the future, she is pointing out that she has not been and still is not one of Boaz's maidservants.

the food: See how this word for food is formed from the same root (אכל) as the verb "to eat?"

Page 31, Ruth 2:14-16
and she caused some to be left: The is the hifil form of the root יתר , which means to remain over. The hifil stem indicates causative action and active voice, so it means the subject of the sentence caused something to be left over. In this case, Ruth did not eat up all her roasted grain. In Isaiah 1:9 the same stem and root appear in the masculine singular perfect form to describe God leaving a remnant with which to rebuild Judah. Exodus 12:10 provides an example of this root used in two different stems in one sentence. The first is a command to not let Passover lamb meat remain till morning, the second describes the leftovers. The first is hifil, causative action and active voice: do not cause leftovers. The second is nifal, passive voice, describing what someone else has left.

to pull you will pull: The absolute infinitive form precedes the conjugated verb for emphasis. Translations have added words like "on purpose," "deliberately," "surely," and "even" to convey Boaz's meaning.

Page 32, Ruth 2:17
about an ephah of: With measurements, a kaf preposition prefix indicates a round number. Biblical measurements call for a translation decision. Modern English readers are unlikely to have an ephah-sized basket in the kitchen, so translators sometimes try to help understanding by not using the transliteration. For example,
it filled an entire basket (NLT)
about 26 quarts of barley (HCSB)
about a week's supply of barley (ISV)
about thirty pounds of barley (NET)
half a bushel (God's Word Translation)
three bushels (Douay-Rheims)
Essentially literal translations (like the KJV and ESV) are more likely to use the transliteration "ephah" and count on the reader to consult references for more information with which to grasp the significance of a measurement.

Page 35, Ruth 2:21
the young men which (are) to me: Hebrew's way of saying "*my young men.*"

Page 36, Ruth 2:23
to be finished: Construct infinitive form of the verb root כלה , to finish.

Page 38, Ruth 3:3
be known: The root ידע means *to know*. Here it is in the passive voice nifal stem, so this verb means *to be known*.

Page 42, Ruth 3:10
you have made good, right: The root יטב means *to be good*. Notice the similarity to the noun and adjective טוב . Here that root is in the hifil stem (causative action, active voice) to show that the subject has caused something to be good, right, and pleasing. In this sentence it is used with a comparison, formed with מִן , between the "last" and "first." Putting it all together, Boaz is saying that Ruth's recent demonstration of steadfast love is even better than the previous one.

Page 43, Ruth 3:12
from me: The prefixed preposition מִ compares the nearness of the other kinsman to Boaz.

Page 45, Ruth 3:14

will be known: As on page 38, at Ruth 3:3, the root ידע is in the passive voice nifal stem, indicating that something is known. Here it appears in the singular, masculine, imperfect tense form.

Page 46, Ruth 3:15

six barleys: Six barleys? Readers of an English translation won't notice anything funny here because translators have added words like "scoops," "measures," "units," or "pounds." But if it was six omers, it wasn't such a grand gift because she gleaned almost twice that much the first day. (1 omer = 1/10 ephah, Exodus 16:36). If it was six ephahs, Boaz loaded up Ruth's garment with something like 225 quarts (215 liters) of grain to carry home. A seah was one-third of an ephah, but six seahs would still leave Ruth with 75 quarts or so of barley to lug back in her cloak. Well, maybe. Jewish commentators of old, reading in Hebrew, noticed the odd phrase and suggested symbolic, prophetic, Messianic possibilities. One is that six barleycorns represented six illustrious descendants of Ruth and Boaz: King David, Daniel, Shadrach, Meshach, Abednego, and Messiah. Rashi's[1] commentary suggested that the six barleycorns hinted at the six attributes mentioned in Isaiah 11:2 of Ruth and Boaz's descendant, the Messiah: the spirit of wisdom and understanding, of counsel and might, of knowledge and fear of the LORD. But then again, why spread out the cloak to receive six little grains? An English translation could leave the text open to such musings by translating this phrase literally as "six barleys" or smooth it out with some assumptions and additional words.

Page 47, Ruth 3:18

he finished: An example of a piel stem pattern verb (intensive action, active voice).

Page 48, Ruth 4:1

a certain someone: Be sure to say this phrase aloud in Hebrew! It is the Biblical Hebrew version of "Mr. So and So" or "such and such." It is used again in the Bible at 2 Kings 6:8 and 1 Samuel 21:3 to refer obliquely to place names. Translations have handled the phrase in Ruth 4:1 variously:
my friend (NIV)
such a one (KJV)
John Doe (NET)
calling him by his name (Douay-Rheims)

Page 54, Ruth 4:10

will be cut off: Nifal stem, imperfect tense conjugation of the root כרת, which means to cut off. Since the nifal pattern indicates the passive voice, this verb means the sentence subject will be cut off, rather than do the cutting. Here it appears negated by לא: the dead man's name will not be cut off.

Page 58, Ruth 4:14

and will be proclaimed: Nifal stem, so the subject (his name) will be proclaimed, not proclaim something.

for restoring soul/life: This same expression is used elsewhere in the Bible. Exploring its range of meanings in other verses can inform your translation of this instance. English Bible translations of this same phrase in Lamentations, Psalms, and Proverbs include: *comfort, encourage, restore strength, refresh strength, preserve life, refresh the soul, relieve the soul, restore the soul, convert the soul.*

Page 59, Ruth 4:16

a supportive caregiver: This word is built on the same root as *amen*. The root's basic meaning is firmness, support, and reliability. This same root is used to describe how Mordecai cared for orphaned Esther (Esther 2:7). It is the word

---

[1] Rashi is an acronym for Rabbi Shlomo Itzhaki, the full, but less commonly used, name of the great medieval Bible and Talmud commentator. Rashi lived in eleventh century France.

translated *foster fathers* in Isaiah 49:23. At Numbers 11:12 it appears in masculine form, referring to an adult carrying a nursing baby. Translators have been divided on what to do with that verse, using variously *nursing father, nurse, foster father, wet nurse, nursing woman,* and *mother.* Here, translations have called Naomi a nurse or foster mother, which might make you wonder what happened to Ruth. This word does not indicate that Naomi took over breastfeeding the baby or raising the child. These days, *nurse* is most likely to mean a medical professional, and we might say instead *nanny* or *caregiver.* But obviously, a grandmother is much more than a nanny. From the surrounding verses, we can see that Obed was certainly a joy and comfort to Naomi, and that she was a loving and involved grandma.

Page 59, Ruth 4:17

born: This root, ילד, appears in the Bible in every verb stem. Here it is in a passive one, pual. Because this is passive, it means that Obed was born. In an active stem, it means to give birth or beget.

Page 60, Ruth 4:17-18

and they called: Notice that the feminine plural Hebrew verb gives information about who called his name Obed that "they" cannot convey. Some translations make it a little clearer than others that the neighbor women named the child. For example, compare the New Living Translation to the English Standard Version:

The neighbor women said, "Now at last Naomi has a son again!" And they named him Obed. (NLT)

And the women of the neighborhood gave him a name, saying, "A son has been born to Naomi." They named him Obed. (ESV)

Obed: This name is built on the familiar root עבד meaning to work, serve, or worship.

fathered: This is ילד in the hifil stem, which indicates causative action and active voice. So Perez caused Hezron to be born, Hezron caused Ram to be born, and so on.

To order Alef Press books and music,
or recommended resources,
and for online tools,
visit us at
www.alefpress.org

www.ingramcontent.com/pod-product-compliance
Lightning Source LLC
Chambersburg PA
CBHW082247300426
44110CB00039B/2459